FEMALE
BODY IMAGE AND
SELF-PERCEPTION

FEMALE
BODY IMAGE AND
SELF-PERCEPTION

LENA KOYA AND MARY-LANE KAMBERG

New York

Published in 2018 by The Rosen Publishing Group, Inc.
29 East 21st Street, New York, NY 10010

Library of Congress Cataloging-in-Publication Data

Names: Koya, Lena, author. | Kamberg, Mary-Lane, author.
Title: Female body image and self-perception / Lena Koya and Mary-Lane Kamberg.
Description: New York: Rosen Publishing, 2018 | Series: Women in the world |
Audience: Grades 7–12. | Includes bibliographical references and index.
Identifiers: ISBN 9781508177265 (library bound) | ISBN 9781508178569 (paperback)
Subjects: LCSH: Body image—Juvenile literature. | Feminine beauty (Aesthetics)—
United States—Juvenile literature. | Self-esteem in women—United States—Juvenile
literature.
Classification: LCC BF724.3.B55 K69 2018 | DDC 306.4'613—dc23

Manufactured in China

CONTENTS

Adolescence can be a very difficult time, particularly for teens who are just developing a sense of self and then learning to accept themselves. In addition to going through physical changes, teens are often dealing with tough issues at school or with friends. They might face pressure from their peers to fit in and pressure from their parents to do well in school. All of these issues, compounded by their first foray into independence from childhood, can lead to issues in self-confidence.

Having self-confidence means that you feel you are a worthwhile person and that you have some value. People who are self-confident might not feel good about themselves all the time, but they do feel confident in their abilities most of the time. Self-confidence is an important foundation to make good decisions and to have the motivation to go after your dreams.

For teen girls, developing self-esteem can be a particularly difficult journey. This is because of many things, including that the media often sends messages to girls and women that they have no value besides their appearance. According to the National

Report on the State of Self-Esteem, a study sponsored by beauty company Dove, 98 percent of girls feel "immense pressure" to look a certain way and 92 percent of girls would like to change the way they look in some way. Often, this immense outside pressure to look a certain way manifests itself in disordered body image. According to author Steven Hinshaw,

The media often sends images to girls and young women suggesting that their only value is in their appearance, which can have devastating effects on their self-esteem.

one in four girls today falls into a clinical diagnosis of depression, eating disorders, cutting, or other mental disorders. This is an upsetting statistic that shows the prevalence of low self-esteem among teenage girls.

In pursuit of the perfection they see in the media, many teenage girls use extreme means—such as starving or cutting themselves—and suffer severe damage to their body image and self-esteem. These behaviors often affect not only a teen's relationship with herself but with others. Teen girls who experience a disordered sense of body image tend to seclude themselves or have difficulty communicating with others. They are less likely to take part in school or community activities and often hesitate to participate in major life events because of their lack of confidence.

While teen girls are disproportionately affected by poor body image, no one is immune. Teen boys also feel extreme pressure to look or act in certain ways, and between 1 and 7 percent of teenage boys suffer from eating disorders. Teens who face additional pressures or feel discriminated against, particularly gay, lesbian, bisexual, and transgender teens, are even more likely to suffer from poor body image, eating disorders, or self-harm such as cutting.

However, this doesn't mean that teens cannot develop a healthier sense of self and higher self-confidence. Experts suggest that focusing on a healthy lifestyle is a good place to start. In addition to a healthy diet, moderate physical activity can also decrease feelings of depression or poor body image. Yet another way is to participate in sports, clubs, and activities. By reaching outside of themselves, many teens can achieve a sense of belonging and community.

Perhaps most important, teens who experience poor body image and depression should reach out for help from trusted mentors, family members, and friends. There is nothing to be ashamed of in asking for help, and often just knowing that others care about you deeply and want to help is enough to take the first step toward greater confidence.

CHAPTER 1

THE MEDIA AND BODY IMAGE

Actress Jennifer Lawrence has enjoyed great success in Hollywood. She is the second-youngest Best Actress Oscar winner in history. For her role as Katniss Everdeen in the Hunger Games series, Lawrence became the highest-grossing action movie heroine of all time. And yet many critics felt the need to comment on Lawrence's weight in the four-film series, instead of focusing on her acting ability alone. Critics said she was "insufficiently malnourished" for her role as a young woman coming from an impoverished district in a dystopian future. They said she had "lingering baby fat" and was a "fairly tall, big-boned lady." The worst: she

Actress Jennifer Lawrence has often spoken out about the ways in which the media unfairly judge young women in Hollywood and their bodies.

was "too big" for her romantic interest, played by Josh Hutcherson. Hutcherson himself is a bulky guy. His character hails from the same impoverished district. Yet no reviewers mentioned his heft.

Lawrence is not the only celebrity condemned by critics. Singer Miley Cyrus has also been attacked for being "fat." She defended herself on Twitter. She posted a photo of a woman with an obvious eating disorder and tweeted, "By calling girls like me fat, this is what you're doing to other people." She also posted a picture of Marilyn Monroe with the tweet, "Proof that you can be adored by thousands of men even when your thighs touch."

Body image is the way you feel about your own physical appearance. A negative body image may include self-criticism of your body, weight, or specific body parts. You might even dislike such things as your hair, skin color, or facial features. The media are largely to blame. Movies, television, music videos, magazines, and advertising bombard young women with messages that "pudgy isn't pretty" and "boys only like thin girls." It's no wonder teenage girls (and those even younger) have trouble with body image.

MEDIA BOMBARDMENT

Today, viewers can turn on their televisions or head to the movies and be bombarded with images

The media, including teen fashion magazines, often idealize an unrealistic body image that few women can achieve.

of very thin models and actresses. Actresses like Natalie Portman and Emily Blunt have felt pressure to restrict their diets in order to be considered for roles. Many other actresses have spoken about the pressure to stay thin in Hollywood, which often means long sessions at the gym and few calories. Contemporary media feature both unrealistically slim actresses and proclaim the dangers of eating disorders at the same time. In 2017, *To the Bone* was released to critical acclaim. Starring Lily Collins, the film explores the danger of anorexia for many young women. Yet, despite the known dangers of eating disorders, the unrealistic Hollywood standard of small waists, long legs, and large busts continues.

Teen magazines keep the bombardment coming. According to the National Institute on Media and the Family, every third article in magazines aimed at teenage girls focuses on appearance. Topics include how to dress, apply makeup, and exercise to remove body flaws. And half of the ads in those magazines appeal to the desire for beauty. They often feature underweight females with muscular males. Photos are touched up, removing wrinkles, fat, and pores so the models look "perfect." The media are sending a false message: beauty brings love, wealth, and happiness. It doesn't.

NOT MEASURING UP

Girls may compare their own bodies with the ones they see in the media. Many come to the conclusion that they don't measure up. They don't realize what models and celebrities do to look perfect. Media darlings need help from personal trainers, stylists, makeup artists, plastic surgeons, and friendly photographers who touch up their images. In reality, they don't really look like their media images.

Girls with a negative body image can become preoccupied with weight and dieting and can even develop eating disorders. They may avoid physical activities, thereby reducing their general fitness. They may lose interest in school. Or, they may harm themselves with alcohol or other drugs or participate in unsafe practices or sexual activity. Their negative body image often leads to low self-esteem.

SELF-ESTEEM

Self-esteem is the way you value yourself. Healthy self-esteem means you accept yourself the way you are. It helps you make friends, develop independence, and challenge yourself—both physically and mentally. On the other hand, low self-esteem has negative effects. Girls as young as in elementary school already see the body as a measure of self-worth.

Girls with low self-esteem lack social skills and avoid social activities. Some suffer from anxiety, depression, or eating disorders. They are generally pessimistic. They fail to recognize their own potential. They minimize their accomplishments. They greet compliments with negativity. Some are afraid to assume responsibilities or form their own opinions.

People with low self-esteem never feel "good enough." They often:

- Think negative thoughts about themselves
- Avoid trying new things
- Compare themselves to others in a negative way
- Have a hard time making friends or participating in social activities
- Feel sad or depressed
- Discount compliments as unwarranted
- Feel jealous
- Put themselves down
- Dwell on past mistakes

Having low self-esteem can change the way people view not only themselves but the world around them. It can be very difficult to feel comfortable and happy when preoccupied with doubts about the way you look.

PUBERTY AND BODY IMAGE

Puberty doesn't help. It's a decidedly awkward stage where everyone—yes, even the most popular girl in school—feels unattractive at times. To make things worse, puberty is a time when girls are most likely to compare themselves with others.

Many girls gain weight as their bodies change shape. Each person's genetic makeup affects this stage of development. Some girls develop "early" compared to their peers. Others develop later. Either way, girls may feel uncomfortable or embarrassed about what their bodies are doing—or not doing. As the body changes, the perceived failure to measure up may become magnified. During puberty—and later—girls have trouble accepting the idea that healthy body shapes vary. Further, puberty is a time of extreme emotions. Low self-esteem at this phase can lead to depression, bad decisions, mental or physical disorders, or suicide.

All this occurs at a time when girls have a strong desire to fit in with peers. Media messages tell them that the way to be accepted is to meet impossible-to-achieve beauty standards and be "hot."

SEXUALIZATION

Overall, the media portray females as sex objects who wear revealing clothes and pose with enticing body posture and facial expressions. Do these visuals offer skewed messages about beauty, health, nutrition, and reality? Many experts say yes.

A task force report from the American Psychological Association (APA) says that sexualization and objectification undermine self-confidence. Sexualization is an emphasis on sexual appeal or behavior in determining self-worth. It places no value at all on other characteristics. Objectification is thinking of or presenting something as an object. In other words, turning a person into an object for another's sexual use.

One major effect of unrealistic media images is the sexualization of girls and young women. Sexualization and objectification have negative effects on important aspects of life. They can lead to such emotional problems as shame and anxiety. The APA also links sexualization with depression, eating disorders, and low self-esteem. And it suggests that sexualization interferes with the development of a healthy sexual self-image.

THE REPRESENTATION PROJECT

In 2011, documentary filmmaker Jennifer Siebel Newsom released *Miss Representation*, which examines the ways in which women and girls are sexualized in the media and the linked issue of the underrepresentation of women and girls in positions of power. The message resonated with the film's viewers. In response to those who asked about harmful representations of boys and men in the media, Newsom made a second film in 2015, titled *The Mask You Live In*, which examines the consequences of toxic masculinity.

Producer Regina Kulik Scully (*left*) and filmmaker
Jennifer Siebel Newsom (*right*) hold up a poster for their film
Miss Representation during its premiere in 2011.

In tandem with these films, Newsom created the Representation Project, a nonprofit that aims to fight media misrepresentation and gender stereotypes. This organization has been at the forefront of many online campaigns to fight harmful stereotypes, including the Ask Her More campaign (#AskHerMore), which encourages reporters to ask female celebrities less about their appearance and more about their accomplishments, and the Not Buying It campaign (#NotBuyingIt), which encourages people to call out sexism in advertising.

BODY CONFIDENCE

Unrealistic images exaggerate the viewer's focus on physical appearance over character, intelligence, humor, compassion, or accomplishment. In real life, women come in a wide variety of shapes and sizes—just like their individual personalities. In fact, only 5 percent of American women have the same "ideal" body type featured in advertising, according to the National Association of Anorexia Nervosa and Associated Disorders (ANAD). Even plus-size models often are thinner than the average woman.

Some companies and organizations are working to reverse this trend. In 2016, Dove, a personal care brand owned by Unilever, conducted a major worldwide study, called "The Dove Global Beauty and Confidence Report." For the report, Dove interviewed 10,500 women from thirteen countries in order to determine how the pressure of unrealistic beauty standards affected their lives. According to this study, low self-esteem has become a challenge most women suffer from—no matter their geographical location or age—with 50 percent of women and girls reporting that they did not often feel comfortable in their own bodies. This was a large drop from a similar study Dove conducted in 2010, which reported that 85 percent of women felt confident about their physical appearance. For girls ages ten to seventeen, 70 percent opted out of major life events because of their lack of confidence, while for women ages eighteen to sixty-four, this percentage rose to 85 percent. These major life events could include trying out for a sports team or spending holidays with family members.

The 2016 study also found that 71 percent of women and 67 percent of girls think the media could do a better job of representing women with a range of physical characteristics and from a range of racial, ethnic, and socioeconomic backgrounds. Other results included:

- 87 percent of women will stop themselves from eating if they are unhappy with the way they look.
- 69 percent of women and 65 percent of girls believe that increased pressure from unrealistic beauty standards shown in the media has contributed to anxiety about their appearance.

The studies conducted by Dove prompted the brand to launch the Campaign for Real Beauty. This advertising campaign used real women without the stereotypical traits that seemed to define beauty in other media. In particular, these Dove advertisements focused on women with "real curves" and different body types, rather than highlighting the typically slender body type often showcased in the media. In 2013, Dove collaborated with the World Association of Girl Guides and Girl Scouts to create Free Being Me. This educational program uses self-esteem boosting sessions and activities to develop pre-teen and teen girls' body confidence. By the end of 2016, the program aimed to reach 3.5 million girls and boys worldwide.

In a different project, the Confidence Coalition promotes self-confidence in girls and women. Created in 2009 by the Kappa Delta Sorority, the group encourages girls and women to "stand up for healthy, balanced, and positive images of girls and women in media." The sorority also created International Girls Day, which is celebrated each year on November 14. Activities for the day encourage girls to build self-confidence. The group hopes the celebration will inspire girls to realize their dreams.

BREAKING HOLLYWOOD STEREOTYPES

Although some celebrities seem to fit into the unrealistic standards set by the media, other celebrities have succeeded in breaking through Hollywood stereotypes. One is Christina Hendricks, best known for her role as Joan Holloway in *Mad Men*, a series that aired on the AMC cable channel from 2007 until 2015. She is a curvy woman, who has been called "a new modern ideal of Hollywood glamour" and a role model for full-figured

Actresses like America Ferrera have helped to break Hollywood stereotypes about what women should look like.

women. She's been compared to such former stars as Marilyn Monroe and Jane Russell. Hendricks has spoken openly about the challenges she has faced for defying Hollywood beauty standards and continues to star in many well-received films, including the 2017 British film *Crooked House*.

America Ferrera is another actress who is helping to change media stereotypes. Early in her career she starred in the film *Real Women Have Curves*. Later, in the lead role in the ABC-TV series *Ugly Betty*, she played a girl with braces, bushy eyebrows, and messy hair instead of a glamorous character. Her work was so well-received that she has won Emmy, Golden Globe, and Screen Actors Guild awards for comedy.

Queen Latifah, an award-winning singer and actress, is another buxom woman whose size has not hindered her success. She has won a Golden Globe Award, an Emmy Award, three Screen Actors Guild Awards, two Image Awards, and a Grammy Award. She has also been nominated for six more Grammys and an Academy Award. She has served as a spokesperson for Cover Girl cosmetics, Curvation ladies underwear, Pizza Hut, and the Jenny Craig weight management company.

Sara Ramirez, who plays orthopedic surgeon Callie Torres *on Grey's Anatomy,* describes herself as "a size twelve in a size zero world." She told *HuffPost Celebrity*:

> "I do understand how there is a teenager somewhere in America who is feeling bad about herself because she has curves. Then she sees a woman who has curves playing a doctor—an intelligent doctor on TV who is flawed and lovable and going through her life just like everybody else—and she identifies with her and feels better about herself. There is the positive side to it too."

CHAPTER 2

BUILDING STRONG RELATIONSHIPS

Off-hand comments about people's weight or other physical attributes can seem harmless. Those who are critical of other people's looks may say they are "just kidding" or are speaking only out of "concern." However, these comments are not only hurtful—they can be harmful as well.

This is because the messages you receive from others—and the ones you send yourself—affect your body image and self-esteem.

Often women are their own worst enemies. In fact, Dove worldwide research found that 54 percent of women say they are their own worst beauty critic. Many young

Building strong relationships is one way to combat poor body image and self-esteem.

women would admit to telling themselves the same hurtful things they are afraid someone else would say to them, such as:

- I'm having a bad hair day.
- My belly sticks out over my jeans waistband.
- I'm too stupid to balance a checkbook.
- My thighs are too fat to go to the pool.

If you're a young woman who is struggling with your own self-esteem, don't contribute to the issue with negative self-talk. It is important to remember to be kind to yourself.

Beyond that, strong social ties are important. Everyone needs the companionship of at least a few good friends they can trust with their secrets and who support them and make them feel included. A good place to start is by becoming your own best friend. Decide that no one has the power to make you feel bad about yourself but you. The next step is to develop a healthy way of communicating with others.

WAYS OF COMMUNICATING

Your body image and self-esteem affect the way you communicate. And the type of communication you use affects your relationships with peers and potential dates. Poor communication styles include submissive, indirect aggression, and direct aggression. They put up barriers to strong, long-term relationships.

Submissive—or passive—communication is characterized by a sense of helplessness. It may be whiny, indecisive, and apologetic. Those who use this style routinely let others make decisions and "go along to get along." They always try to please others, consider others' needs ahead of themselves, and prefer not to make waves. It's easy to see how low self-esteem encourages this type of communication. But it's ineffective in letting others know your needs, wants, and opinions.

People using indirect aggression may be sarcastic, deceptive, and manipulative. They send mixed messages and try to induce guilt in others. Indirect aggression is a defense mechanism they use to protect themselves and ward off attacks from others. Again, however, it is a poor way to interact.

Finally, direct aggression comes across as bossy, arrogant, opinionated, and overbearing. It's a way to get your own way every time and gain control over another person. Bullying falls into the category of direct aggression.

BULLYING

Girls with low self-esteem often are victims of bullies. Bullying is abusive, intentional cruelty. It is a type of aggression that includes an imbalance of power, repetition, and intent to harm physically or mentally. It's a social relationship problem.

Sometimes bullying takes the form of nasty rumors, breaking confidences, and getting others to dislike the victim. Most hurtful may be behaviors that range from simple rejection to complete exclusion from a social group. Bullying behaviors may include name-calling, teasing, or spreading rumors. These may escalate to threats, vandalism, leers and stares, and assault and battery. In high schools, bullying often takes the form of sexual harassment. Behaviors may include comments about a person's body, inappropriate touching, slurs about sexual orientation, and sexual assault.

Today's technology offers easy tools for bullies. Cyberbullying is sending embarrassing, false, or other harmful messages or images over the internet, mobile phones, or other devices. Common examples

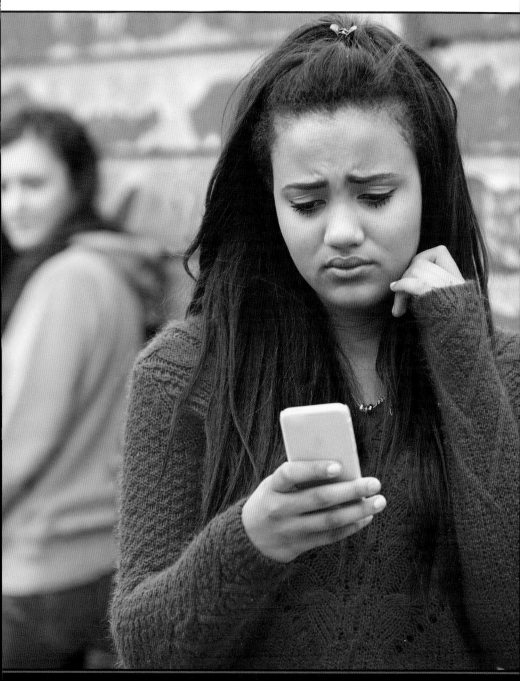

Bullying—and particularly cyberbullying—is rampant. Many teens admit to having been negatively affected by bullying at some point during their lives.

are excessive emails, texts, instant messages, or postings to social network pages. Cyberbullies may ridicule another, make false comments in the person's name, or send digital pornographic material. Some cyberbullies use social media to recruit others to join in the bullying.

Bullying of all types is rampant. Some have called it a national epidemic. And no wonder. According to StompOutBullying.com, 35 percent of teens say they have been victims of bullying. And 15 percent of youth have been bullied online.

At the stage of life when others' opinions matter the most, teens who are bullied can experience loneliness, emotional distress, and severe damage to their body image and self-esteem. Some stay home from school because of it. In fact, 160,000 students stay home from school every day because of bullying, according to the National Education Association. Some beg to change schools. Some consider or commit suicide.

WHY BULLIES BULLY

Victims may be surprised to learn the reasons teens bully. One of the biggest reasons is the same desire to fit in that their victims have. Bullies gossip because they don't want to be left out of the group. They bully because others are doing it. And they bully to get "respect" from their peers. Some say they do it to punish people they are jealous of or to feel better about themselves by putting others down.

Another prevalent reason teens bully is to alleviate boredom and create excitement. In short, they think it's fun. They spread rumors or embellish tales from weekend parties and enjoy the attention they get from being part of the "popular" group. They are desperate to belong. In reality, they have serious low self-esteem issues themselves. Like their victims, they feel vulnerable and unsure of themselves.

BORN THIS WAY

Pop star Lady Gaga understands. In high school, a group of students stuffed her into a trashcan. She pretended to laugh along, but the truth is it hurt. She never told her parents or other adults. But when a fan committed suicide, she came to realize that school-age kids still suffer from bullying today. She made a commitment to help stop it.

The high-profile singer, who has sold 27 million albums and 146 million singles, used her celebrity capital, as well as $1.2 million in cash, to establish the Born This Way Foundation in 2012. Its purpose is to help young people who are suffering from bullying and self-confidence issues. This includes both bullies and victims. At the launch of the foundation, reported

34

Lady Gaga created the Born This Way Foundation in 2012 to help young people combat bullying and self-esteem issues. The foundation has since established several programs to deter online bullying in particular.

on Slate.com, she said, "There's all this focus on the victims, but the bullies are on the same playing field. They both need our help."

The foundation has teamed with the Harvard Graduate School of Education and the Berkman Center for Internet & Society to create a "new culture of kindness, bravery, acceptance, and empowerment." The MacArthur Foundation, which supports efforts to build a more peaceful world, also supports the foundation. It issued a $500,000 grant to support online and in-person programs to deter bullying and engage young people to work to stop meanness and cruelty. In 2016, the Born This Way Foundation partnered with technology group Intel and media outlets Vox Media and Re/code to fight online harassment.

BE ASSERTIVE!

Some people think that being assertive is the same as being aggressive. However, assertive communication is the most useful way to speak—as well as listen—to others. It breaks down barriers between people.

Assertive communication expresses both positive and negative feelings in an open, direct way. People using this style respect the rights of others. They also respect their own. They avoid judging or blaming others. And they work to solve conflicts in ways acceptable to everyone involved. The goal is to get others to treat them with respect by demonstrating that they respect themselves.

One way to do that is to use positive messages when you think and talk about yourself. In addition, avoid qualifying remarks that minimize what you're trying to say. Avoid saying such things as "that's just my idea," "if it's all right with you," or "is that OK?" Don't feel the need to explain your choices. And don't apologize for your feelings or ideas. Assertive communication helps you express your needs and feelings. It eliminates the need to read another person's mind or to expect someone to read yours.

Another technique is to use "I" messages that include a statement of another's behavior, your feeling about it, and the effect on yourself when others act a certain way. For example:

- "You make me angry" becomes "I feel angry when you …"
- "You're always late" becomes "I feel unimportant when you're late."
- "I think you…" becomes "I feel frustrated when …"

Assertive communication eliminates the need to take responsibility for others' feelings or behaviors. Avoid "you should," "ought to," or "have to." Replace them with "I choose to …"

When you want something, use three steps. First say something that honors the other person's feelings, such as "I know you feel frustrated when…" Next, clearly state the problem and tell how you feel when it happens. Finally, clearly state what you want or what you want to see changed.

Some additional tips include:

- Make eye contact.
- Stand or sit straight.
- Smile.
- Use facts, not judgments.

These techniques can help you communicate your needs assertively and firmly, while also remaining kind and sympathetic. It is a great way to build up your own self-confidence, too.

One of the most troubling issues for teens with low self-esteem is dating. Teens should make sure their partner treats them well and that they have a solid foundation of self-esteem before becoming attached to someone else.

SELF-ESTEEM AND DATING

One of the most troubling issues for teens with poor body image and low self-esteem revolves around dating. Teens who think they're not good-looking enough or thin enough may put off potential dates with such self-conscious body language as crossed arms and slumped shoulders. Other teens base their self-worth on whether they have a mate. They are so desperate for a romantic partner to make them feel accepted that they settle for a relationship that fails to offer true respect and appreciation.

Issues concerning body image, self-esteem, and dating are just one more way teens let others define how they value themselves. Low self-esteem can also lead to teen promiscuity. Sex becomes a way to build confidence and feel loved, accepted, desired, and—yes—

beautiful. Unfortunately, it also puts teens at risk for sexually transmitted diseases as well as mental, physical, or sexual abuse.

VICTIMS OF ABUSE

Abuse is behavior aimed at getting power and control over another person. The behavior may be mental, physical, or sexual. The abuser has little or no concern for the victim's needs. And victims often live with constant fear. They lose feelings of safety and security. Abuse that occurs in childhood and teen years often follows the victim to adulthood. There, the damage from abuse affects lifelong friendships and sexual relationships.

Female abuse victims often accept some false beliefs:

- People wouldn't like me if they knew the "real" me.
- I need a partner to protect me and make me whole.
- Avoiding conflict is more important than standing up for myself.
- I should not express anger.
- I deserve the treatment I am receiving.

- My public image is more important than my health, safety, or self-esteem.
- Others' needs and feelings are more important than mine.

Some girls and women who believe these ideas need professional help to learn the role they play in the abuse cycle and how to change it. The good news is that they can learn how changing their behavior and view of themselves can break the cycle of abuse. They can learn that they can—and need to—take care of themselves and take responsibility for their own feelings. They can define themselves instead of giving that power to others. And they can revise their view of conflict and learn to stand up for themselves.

If you find yourself in an abusive situation of any kind, seek help from a school nurse, counselor, or social worker. Or, contact the abuse hotline in your state. You can also ask for help from a trusted adult or clergyperson. These resources can help refer you to professionals trained to treat victims of abuse. You can also call domestic abuse hotlines. For severe sexual abuse or rape, call the police.

MYTHS AND
FACTS

Myth: Cyberbullying is less damaging than traditional bullying.

Truth: In the age of social media, cyberbullying can have devastating consequences. In some ways, cyberbullying can be more harmful than traditional bullying because there is no way for a victim to escape it without completely disconnecting from technology.

Myth: Abuse typically only occurs in "problem" families, or among poorer or uneducated social groups.

Fact: Anyone can be abused, regardless of race, gender, ethnicity, geographical location, or socioeconomic status. Those who have more financial independence are just as likely to become the victim of abuse as those who come from poorer backgrounds. Social and economic factors do not dictate who will become an abuser; rather it is an internal feeling of power over others.

Myth: Your self-confidence will increase if you lose weight or otherwise change your body.

Fact: Self-confidence is not completely dictated by outside factors but also by internal feelings regarding one's own self-worth. Some people have supposedly "ideal" bodies and still struggle with poor body image. It is important to change how you perceive yourself—not how others perceive you—in order to cultivate better self-confidence.

EATING DISORDERS AND SELF-HARM

Low self-esteem can have serious consequences for teens' mental and physical health. In fact, low body confidence is linked with many serious health conditions, including eating disorders. In addition to being more at risk for eating disorders, teens with low self-esteem are more likely to engage in self-destructive behaviors such as cutting. These behaviors can lead to severe bodily harm and even death.

An eating disorder is a life-threatening condition that involves serious physical and emotional problems along with attitudes and behaviors concerning weight and

In severe circumstances, low self-esteem can lead to eating disorders. Anorexia nervosa is the most common—and the deadliest—eating disorder and affects many teens.

food. It is a form of addiction that is as hard to conquer as addictions to alcohol, nicotine, and other drugs. The most common eating disorders are anorexia nervosa, bulimia nervosa, and binge eating disorder (BED).

ANOREXIA NERVOSA

Anorexia nervosa is a medical diagnosis characterized by starvation. It is the most common and deadliest eating disorder. It often includes some of the following symptoms:

- Excessive influence of body weight on body image or self-esteem
- Obsessive desire to be thinner
- Inability to maintain body weight at the normal range for age and height
- Significant weight loss
- Abnormal menstrual cycle or complete cessation
- Extreme dieting

According to Eating Disorder Hope, between 1 and 4.2 percent of women have suffered from anorexia during their lifetime, while .3 percent of men suffer from the disease. Anorexia has the highest rate of mortality of any mental illness. It is estimated that 4 percent of those who suffer from anorexia will die from related complications, including cardiac arrest and failure of other organs.

For females with anorexia between the ages of fifteen and twenty-four, the mortality rate is twelve times greater than the death rate from all other causes of death in that age group, according to the National Association of Anorexia Nervosa and Associated Disorders.

Anorexia literally means loss of appetite. However, anorexics often are very hungry most of the time, especially early in the process of developing the disorder. They feel better about themselves when they can overcome hunger and control what and how much they eat.

BULIMIA NERVOSA

Bulimia nervosa may occur by itself or in conjunction with anorexia nervosa. Like anorexics, teens with bulimia are trying to control their feelings. Bulimia means "ox-hunger." Bulimics eat huge amounts of food in a short period of time—even when they are not hungry. Then they purge.

Purging is a way to get rid of recently eaten food to keep from gaining weight. It may appear as skipped meals, excessive exercise, self-induced vomiting, or taking laxatives, enemas, or diuretics. However, it's also a way to express feelings of anger, stress, depression, or anxiety. Sometimes a dentist is the first to notice bulimic symptoms. Stomach acid from frequent vomiting erodes tooth enamel. It also damages gums, turns teeth brown, or causes sores in the mouth.

Other symptoms of bulimia nervosa include:

- Use of body weight as a measure of one's value as a person
- Hiding food or eating in secret
- Frequent dieting
- Repeated episodes of binge eating followed by purging
- Lack of control while eating

Some bulimics engage in these behaviors as a way to punish themselves for unrealistic guilt. Genetic factors as well as environmental ones may be involved in the development of the disorder.

BINGE EATING DISORDER

Binge eating disorder (BED) is excessive overeating. In fact, it was once known as compulsive overeating. It often is associated with obesity. According to Eating Disorder Hope, about 3 percent of American adults will suffer from BED during their lifetime. However, they don't compensate with purging. They may have a long history of dieting that didn't work. Genetics may predispose them to be larger or heavier than their average peers.

Some symptoms of BED include:

- Frequently eating large amounts of food in a short period
- Inability to stop eating
- Eating fast or in secret
- Feeling too full after binge eating

Teens with BED often feel ashamed or embarrassed. They sometimes eat too much because they're so hungry from dieting or other food restrictions. Or, they eat too much to comfort themselves. The overeating helps them ignore their feelings or avoid uncomfortable situations. BED is often associated with depression.

Although different types of eating disorders seem to have specific symptoms, the illnesses vary widely. A single individual may from time to time exhibit behavior and attitudes that cross the lines among them. Another category called eating disorders not otherwise specified (EDNOS) includes combinations of signs and symptoms of the other three. Defining the type of eating disorder is not as important as recognizing that a person's extreme relationship with food may have exceeded the normal range and become a mental or physical illness.

TRANSGENDER TEENS AND EATING DISORDERS

According to a 2015 study published in the *Journal of Adolescent Health*, transgender teens have the highest risk of developing eating disorders of any group. About 16 percent of transgender teens report having been diagnosed with an eating disorder in the past year. Transgender teens also reported a higher usage of diet pills than other groups at 13.5 percent. Compare this with the nearly 4.5 percent of heterosexual teen girls who report using diet pills.

One reason researchers believe that transgender teens are at a higher risk of developing eating disorders is because of the stress and discrimination they face as transgender individuals. One researcher wrote,

> "Minority stress has been identified as a potential factor in the association between transgender and disordered eating. Among lesbian, gay, and bisexual individuals, a strong link has been found between higher levels of minority stress and poorer mental health outcomes. The same mechanisms are likely at play in transgender individuals, who may be exposed to substantial amounts of discrimination, both on an interpersonal and societal level."

WHO GETS EATING DISORDERS?

People of all genders, races, ethnicities, and ages can suffer from eating disorders. The distribution of the illness ranges from the age of six to seventy-six. The National Association of Anorexia Nervosa and Associated Disorders estimates that at least thirty million people suffer from an eating disorder in the United States. However, accurate statistics are difficult to obtain because those with eating disorders tend to hide their problems and behaviors.

First symptoms usually appear in adolescence. While some genetic factors may be involved, such environmental events as the death of a loved one, exposure to violence, school-related stress, and peer pressure often trigger their development. People who are perfectionists are at higher risk than others. They create such unrealistic expectations for themselves that they experience frequent disappointment. Researchers have found no link between eating disorders and race or the individual's occupation, education, or socio-economic status.

HIGH-PROFILE SUFFERERS

Several celebrities who have suffered from eating disorders have come forward to build awareness of the issue. Those who suffer from eating disorders often can

Eating disorders affect a broad range of people regardless of gender, race, or ethnicity, although symptoms usually first appear during adolesence.

also have other addictions to drugs or alcohol, such as Russell Brand. Many also engage in other forms of self-inflicted harm, such as Demi Lovato.

DEMI LOVATO

Singer and songwriter Demi Lovato has spoken publically about her struggles with bulimia as well as her tendency to harm herself. In an interview with *American Way* magazine, Lovato speaks about how, as a young girl, she experienced her mother and grandmother's struggle with bulimia. "Even though I was two or three years old," Lovato states. "Being around somebody who was 80 pounds [36 kilograms] and had an active eating disorder … it's hard not to grow up like that." Later, when Lovato was just nine years old, she began a pattern of binging and purging. Around this time she also began cutting herself, largely in response to being bullied in school.

Singer and songwriter Demi Lovato has often spoken out about her struggles with poor body image, bulimia, and her tendency to harm herself. She hopes to dissuade her fans from engaging in these destructive habits.

53

After spending time in rehab for addictive behavior in 2010 at the age of twenty-one, Lovato has rebounded and speaks often about her past struggles. She tries to raise awareness about the dangers of eating disorders and other forms of self-harm among her young fans. "When I have meet-and-greets, I can't tell you the amount of times that girls will show me their arms covered in scars or cuts," Lovato states. "They'll tell me, 'You helped me get through this. Because of you, I stopped self harming …' Hearing those things gave my life new meaning."

LILY COLLINS

Actress Lily Collins drew attention to the plight of those who suffer from eating disorders in 2017 with her role in *To The Bone*, a movie about a young woman suffering from anorexia. For Collins, the role was almost too familiar to her. She, too, suffered from anorexia for years before recovering fully in 2007.

In an interview with IMDB Studio, Collins explained why she thought it was necessary to play a role that might bring up her past struggles. "This was definitely a more dramatic role for me. I suffered with eating disorders when I was a teenager as well," she said. "[When I got the script] it was like the universe putting these things in my sphere to help me face, kind of dead on, a fear that I used to have." It was difficult, she continued, having to relive some of her past painful experiences while preparing for the role and working with eating disorder specialists on set.

But, Collins, explained, "Sharing my history with eating disorders and how personal this film has been is one of the most fulfilling experiences of my life ... [To those who suffer from eating disorders] remember that you are never alone."

OPRAH WINFREY

Oprah Winfrey, possibly the most successful and best-known woman in the American television industry, has often spoken about her eating disorders, which include BED. She has said that food comforted her, and being heavy made her feel safe. However, she lost several jobs for being too overweight. And she had several bad relationships with men that she blames on her need for approval.

She told her own *O Magazine*, "Getting my

Talk show host, producer, and actress Oprah Winfrey has also publically discussed her struggles with poor body image and weight loss in order to help her fans.

lifelong weight struggle under control has come from a process of treating myself as well as I treat others in every way."

SELF-INJURY

In some cases people use another approach to express emotions, relieve pain, or punish themselves for real or imagined flaws or actions. The broad disorder is known as self-injury or self-mutilation. It includes cutting, hair-pulling, self-hitting, bone-breaking, and burning. Whatever the means, the goal is to harm one's body.

The pain makes those who engage in self-injury feel better. Relief comes from the body's release of beta-endorphin. Beta-endorphin is a naturally occurring chemical produced in the brain's pituitary gland. It has better pain-killing properties than the narcotic pain reliever morphine. The body releases it in response to pain, trauma, exercise, or stress.

Cutting is the most common form of self-injury. Cutters use such tools as knives, razor blades, broken glass, or scissors to make shallow slices in the skin. Some make multiple cuts. Others make only one or two. Cutters are not trying to commit suicide. However, they can die if they accidentally cut too deeply and sever an artery. Accidents are more likely if the cutter is under the influence of alcohol or other drugs and unable to feel pain or recognize a severe injury.

Another form of self-injury is hair pulling, also known as trichotillomania. The hair puller pulls hair from the scalp, eyebrows, eyelashes, or other parts of the body. Some take a lot of hair at one time. Others take only a few, but repeat the behavior all day. Sometimes the hair does not grow back.

Self-hitting and bone breaking involve striking oneself with an object or slamming part of the body against a wall or the floor. In some cases the strikes are hard enough to break one's own arm, leg, or wrist. Burning is damage to the skin with a match, candle, or other fire source. It also includes heating a metal instrument like a paper clip, fork, or knife and pressing it onto the skin.

Inability to deal with emotions is associated with self-injury disorders. The behaviors are ways to cope with anger, rejection, failure, loss, or helplessness. The person often feels a sense of control from the activity, but strives to keep the injuries secret by hiding scars under long sleeves or long pants.

GETTING HELP

Reaching out for help is difficult, whether it's for oneself or a friend. A good place to start is with parents, a primary care doctor, religious counselor, or

Teens who struggle with poor self-esteem, disordered eating, or self-destructive behavior should first reach out to a trusted friend, family member, family care doctor, or social worker.

school nurse or social worker. Teens who feel they need to reach out to someone can also call hotlines for eating disorders, self-injury, and suicide.

If you suspect a friend of having one of these issues, approach him or her with kindness. Never ignore talk of suicide, even if you think your friend is joking. Tell a trusted adult right away.

In discussing possible eating or self-injury disorders, point out specific behaviors you have noticed. Explain the behaviors in terms of the symptoms of the specific illness. Emphasize that your friend may have a health problem that requires medical attention. Avoid accusing, shaming, or embarrassing your friend. And refrain from diagnosis—that's a professional's job. Instead encourage your friend to seek help.

The earlier someone gets help for an eating disorder or self-injury problem, the better the chances of reversing its physical and emotional damage. A big roadblock, though, is the fact that people with addictions often want to keep them. They fear losing the sense of control the disorder gives them. In a way, they feel safe with their harmful behaviors. So, even if they acknowledge a problem, they resist getting help for it.

Most people with these disorders need the help of medical or mental health professionals. These caregivers help patients discover the underlying causes of the illness and find healthy coping tools. They also guide the patient on a process of self-discovery that helps restore body image and self-esteem.

Treatment often lasts a year or more and may include psychotherapy, counseling, and self-help groups. In many cases, the entire family is involved in the process. In severe cases of life-threatening symptoms, hospitalization may be necessary. No drugs have been approved for treating eating disorders. However, some antidepressants may hold promise for treating the underlying causes of eating disorders.

HEALTHY LIFESTYLES

Many teens have a complicated relationship with food, even if they do not fit the criteria for having an eating disorder. The term "disordered eating" describes any of these abnormal eating patterns that teens might engage in, such as binge eating without purging, compulsive eating after experiencing emotional stressors, or restricted eating to lose weight or in certain social situations.

Disordered eating may involve symptoms of anorexia, bulimia, or other diagnoses, so it's hard to tell them apart. Although disordered eating is considered less serious than full-blown eating disorders, it can still harm the body. At the least, it signals food or body image issues. A good way to tell which category the unusual eating pattern falls into is to examine

A healthy and balanced diet, as well as moderate exercise, is important for a healthy lifestyle.

motives and symptoms in terms of body image and self-esteem and the emotions that surround them.

Disordered eating might include cutting back on calories the day or two after a huge meal. Doing that to balance out calories is one thing. But if you do it because you feel guilty for having eaten too much—or for eating at all— you could be headed for trouble. Guilt, shame, or other emotional distress about what you're doing is a warning sign.

How often does the new pattern occur? If you eat too much on holidays or special occasions during the year, the behavior might be considered relatively isolated overindulgence. But if you overeat on a regular basis, you may be approaching the line between disordered eating and eating disorder. Eating behavior that causes physical harm is always suspect. However, many people with eating disorders fail to see what is happening to their bodies until the damage is severe.

Yo-yo dieting may also be considered disordered eating. Yo-yo dieting is a pattern of dieting to lose weight followed by regaining the weight—or more—then dieting again. The diets restrict calories so much that the body reduces its rate of metabolism and goes into starvation mode.

Metabolism is the total of the body's chemical processes for growth, energy production, waste material elimination, and more. A slower metabolism contributes to regaining the weight once you return to a normal eating pattern. Yo-yo dieting also harms self-esteem. The person may feel like a failure for being unable to maintain a steady weight.

If you want to feel healthy, strong, and confident, a good way to start is with proper nutrition and appropriate physical activity. That's just what Queen Latifah encourages. As a celebrity client for the Jenny Craig weight management company in 2008 and 2009, Queen Latifah's message was losing weight for better health, not to get skinny.

Achieving her weight-loss goal meant that her clothes fit better. And she had more energy. Most important to her, fans realized that her efforts were for health reasons, not an attempt to fit into a stereotyped look or size.

A HEALTHY DIET

Moderation and variety are the keys to healthy eating habits. The purpose of a food plan is to ensure that your body gets the nutrients it needs within a daily calorie goal for weight loss, weight gain, or weight maintenance. The benefits include lower risk of heart disease, diabetes, and cancer. Try to eat different

A healthy diet consists mostly of vegetables and grains, with smaller amounts of meats and fat and little to no sugar.

foods each week to ensure a good balance of vitamins and minerals.

So what should you eat? According to the National Heart Lung and Blood Institute, a healthy diet emphasizes fruits, vegetables, whole grains, and fat-free or low-fat dairy products. Protein sources include lean meat, poultry, and fish, as well as beans, eggs, and nuts. Portion size is important. A typical serving of meat, for example, should be about the size of the palm of your hand. A healthy food plan also minimizes intake of saturated fats, trans fat, cholesterol, salt, and added sugar.

A healthy diet has a good balance of carbohydrates, protein, and fat. According to Becky Hand, a licensed and registered dietitian, carbohydrates should comprise 45 percent to 65 percent of daily calories. Protein should contribute 10 percent to 35 percent. And the remaining 20 percent to 35 percent should come from fat.

TYPES OF FATS

Everyone needs some fat in the diet. Without it your body can't use the vitamins A, D, E, or K. They are fat-soluble, which means they dissolve only in fat. Fat is a source of heat and energy. It also pads and insulates nerves and organs. The four main types of fat are monounsaturated fat, polyunsaturated fat, saturated fat, and trans fat. Saturated and trans fats may be harmful to one's health and are solid at room temperature. Monounsaturated and polyunsaturated dietary fats are liquid at room temperature and may actually be quite beneficial to one's health.

MONOUNSATURATED FAT

Monounsaturated fat helps decrease the risk of heart disease and controls insulin levels and blood sugar. It is found in avocados and nuts, as well as in olive, peanut, and canola oils. Doctors recommend getting most of your daily fat calories from monounsaturated instead of saturated fat.

POLYUNSATURATED FAT

Polyunsaturated fat comes mostly from plant-based foods and oils, especially corn, soybean, and sunflower oils. It also is found in fish oil. Polyunsaturated fat reduces the risks of heart disease and diabetes. There are two kinds of polyunsaturated fat: omega-3 and omega-6 fatty acids.

As fat breaks down, it releases fatty acids in the forms the body needs. Omega-3 and omega-6 fatty acids contribute to normal growth and development. They also help prevent obesity, bone loss, high cholesterol, high blood pressure, diabetes, cancer, depression, and other health problems. However, omega-6 fatty acids can contribute to inflammation

Foods like salmon, sardines, and walnuts are high in polyunsatured fats and have many health benefits.

while omega-3 fatty acids do not. This is why doctors suggest maximizing omega-3 fatty acids in your diet over omega-6 fatty acids.

The body makes most of the fatty acids it needs from fruits and vegetables. However, the body cannot make its own omega-3 and omega-6 fatty acids. The body must get them from the food you eat. Good sources of omega-3 fatty acids include salmon, tuna, halibut, mackerel, lake trout, herring, sardines, and other seafood. The American Heart Association recommends eating fish at least twice a week. You can also get omega-3 fatty acids from soybeans, pumpkin seeds, nut oils, soybean oil, olive oil, and garlic. Omega-6 fatty acids are found mostly in sardines, poultry, soybean oil, sunflower oil, walnuts, and pecans.

SATURATED FAT

Saturated fat comes mainly from animal food sources and causes health concerns about heart disease and diabetes. Many people think that all saturated fat comes from animal sources. Much of it does. Examples include beef, pork, poultry, whole milk, butter, cheese, and lard. However such vegetable sources as coconut oil and palm oil also contain mostly saturated fat. A healthy diet gets 10 percent or less of its calories from saturated fats.

TRANS FAT

Trans fat also comes from animal food sources. However, most of it comes from a type of food processing called partial hydrogenation of unsaturated fats. Trans fat also is known as industrial or synthetic trans fat. It's easier to cook with and less likely to spoil than its natural counterpart. But like its saturated cousin, it poses health risks for heart disease. Doctors recommend eating as few trans fats as possible.

LOSING WEIGHT THE HEALTHY WAY

If you are overweight for your age, height, and build, losing weight can have health benefits. The formula is easy. You need to use more calories than you take in. If you use the same number of incoming and outgoing calories, your weight will stay the same. If you eat more calories than you use, you'll gain.

According to the National Heart, Lung, and Blood Institute, to lose one to two pounds per week, reduce your daily intake by 500 to 1,000 calories. In general, eating plans with 1,200 to 1,500 calories per day are safe for female weight loss. If you are hungry when you are on a reduced calorie diet, increase the daily number of calories by 100 to 200.

Diets using very low calorie counts of 800 calories or less should be used only with a doctor's supervision.

THE IMPORTANCE OF EXERCISE

A weight loss plan works best if a plan for healthy exercise accompanies it. Unfortunately, some teens with poor body image or low self-esteem avoid sports altogether. Or, they participate and risk developing eating disorders. Some teens resist physical activity. Others exercise too much. As with other aspects of body image and self-esteem, the right amount of exercise depends on the reasons for doing it.

According to the Confidence Coalition, 40 percent of girls between the ages of eleven and seventeen avoid sports because of a lack of skills. Of course, skills can be learned. You can be born with a natural talent for sports, music, or visual art. But you must develop those talents by learning the skills for those activities.

A healthy exercise program focuses on health, not weight loss. It's part of a rewarding lifestyle. You can choose from a wide variety of activities from organized sports to working alone. Some teens like the shared companionship of team sports. Others prefer individual sports like swimming or tennis or noncompetitive activities like biking or snowboarding.

In choosing an activity, keep in mind that the best exercise is the one you'll do. If it feels like a chore, you'll likely drop out. If it's fun, you'll stay at it.

ENDURANCE, STRENGTH, AND FLEXIBILITY

A healthy body has three elements: endurance, strength, and flexibility. All three are important to your fitness. You build endurance with aerobic exercise. Aerobic exercise is any activity that quickens your breathing and heart rate. It is called aerobic because it involves the systems that deliver oxygen to the body. Activities that build endurance include swimming, running, biking, hiking, and fast walking.

Strength training also contributes to endurance. The stronger your muscles, the longer you can exercise without getting worn out. Strength training also helps athletes in many sports develop enough strength to perform required skills. Strong muscles also prevent injury by supporting the joints involved in athletic

Practicing yoga can increase strength and flexbility. It can also reduce stress and be an enjoyable way of maintaining a healthy lifestyle.

movement. Examples of strength training include such weight-bearing exercises as pull-ups, push-ups, crunches, squats, and leg-raises. Sports that develop strength include rowing, cross-country skiing, biking, and skating.

Flexibility means that you can stretch or bend with ease. It protects the body from muscle strains and sprains and improves athletic performance. Stretching exercises encourage flexibility. Activities that increase flexibility include martial arts, ballet, gymnastics, and yoga. After any type of exercise, it's good to perform stretching exercises specific to the arms, legs, back, and neck.

THE BENEFITS OF EXERCISE

With good health as the motivating factor, exercise increases the physical and mental aspects of your life. Here are some of the benefits of physical activity:

- Exercise feels good. That's because it releases the same pain-killing endorphins some people seek from negative activities like cutting and hair pulling.
- Exercise improves attitude. The feeling of accomplishment from achieving sports or fitness goals helps raise self-esteem.
- Fitness improves physical appearance. It helps you reach and maintain a healthy weight.

- Exercise improves overall health. It reduces risk factors for such diseases as high blood pressure, type 2 diabetes, and heart disease.

EATING DISORDERS AND SPORTS

Although it is important to remain active for your health, sometimes too much or too little exercise are symptoms of eating disorders. Girls with a poor body image often avoid sports because they fear they'll look bad in the uniform. This is especially true in "appearance sports," where the body is on display. Examples include swimming, figure skating, and gymnastics. Girls who participate in these types of sports have a greater risk of developing eating disorders. According to Eating Disorder Hope, 42 percent of female athletes who participate in appearance sports demonstrate eating disordered behavior. Eating disorders are also prevalent among elite athletes. Again according to Eating Disorder Hope, 13.5 percent of athletes have eating disorders compared with 3 percent of the general population.

THE FEMALE ATHLETE TRIAD

A combination of three interrelated conditions common among female athletes is known as the female athlete triad. A girl with the triad constantly feels tired, has trouble sleeping, and often has cold

Gymnasts have a higher risk of developing the female athlete triad, a group of interelated conditions including lack of energy, menstrual cycle disturbance, and bone loss.

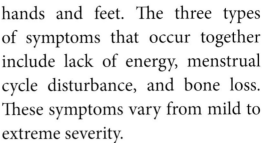

hands and feet. The three types of symptoms that occur together include lack of energy, menstrual cycle disturbance, and bone loss. These symptoms vary from mild to extreme severity.

Athletes need the energy from food for peak performance. In girls with the triad, low energy results from using more calories than they eat. Some athletes consciously restrict the amount of food in an effort to look thin or perform better. And sometimes this eating pattern evolves into anorexia or bulimia.

Irregular menstrual cycles can result from excessive exercise. If the athlete skips her menstrual period for three months or longer (and she's not pregnant), she has a potentially serious problem called amenorrhea.

Athletes who have the triad also risk losing bone mass. This can lead to weakened bones. The athlete may suffer stress fractures or broken bones. Over time she may develop osteoporosis, a condition where bones become brittle from loss of protein and minerals, notably calcium.

RISK FACTORS

Being a gymnast, figure skater, ballet dancer, distance runner, swimmer, or diver may place too much emphasis on a lean figure. Such athletes are at risk for developing the triad. Other risk factors include:

- Participating in such sports as boxing that require weight checks.
- Attending so many sporting events that they interfere with social life.
- Exercising beyond normal workouts for the sport.
- Feeling pressure to win no matter what.
- Feeling—or being—punished for gaining weight.
- Dealing with controlling coaches and/or parents.

Teens who participate in weight-class sports such as wrestling are also at a much higher risk of suffering from an eating disorder. This is because these athletes are frequently weighed in order to maintain a particular weight class for matches. Many weight-class athletes, including wrestlers, rowers, and martial arts athletes, feel pressure from their coaches or teammates to lose weight quickly, which can lead to disordered eating and excessive exercising.

It's not always easy to figure out if you are eating a healthy diet according to your own individual needs. Here are ten great questions to ask a dietician in order to make sure your health and fitness is on track:

1. How many calories should I be eating for my age, sex, and height?

2. What is the correct portion size for meats, carbohydrates, and vegetables?

3. Is it unhealthy to eat a dessert every day?

4. What are some healthy foods I should be eating every day?

5. If I need to lose weight, how should I adjust my diet?

6. How much exercise should I be getting every week?

7. Am I at risk for developing an eating disorder?

8. Is it ok to engage in "emotional eating"?

9. How can I develop a healthier relationship with food?

10. What is the best piece of nutritional advice you can give?

CHAPTER 5

SUCCESS AND SELF-CONFIDENCE

Being successful in life—whatever that means to you—depends on having the confidence to go out and get what you want and deserve. This means going for a sports team, a college, and eventually a job. Those who "put themselves out there" are people with confidence and high self-esteem. That's why it's important to develop body confidence early on.

One way to develop self-confidence is to try to step back and look at yourself objectively. Use positive self-talk instead of criticisms. Refrain from such self-talk as "I don't matter," "Nobody likes me," or "I'm not good enough." Instead, make a

Self-confidence puts you on a path to success, whether that means doing well in school, making a sports team, or getting that perfect job.

conscious choice to send encouraging messages: "I can do this." "I'm a good person." "If I make mistakes, I'll try again." Whenever bad thoughts creep in, replace them with something positive.

Make three lists: what you like to do, what you're good at, and what you'd like to do (now or in the future). Add to the lists as you think of more items. Focus on the things you're good at. You might be surprised how many things you do well.

Low self-esteem often comes from a fear of failure. What better way to overcome that fear than to prove yourself wrong? Focus on what you're good at instead of dwelling on your past mistakes. Set realistic, specific goals and work toward them. When you succeed, celebrate the achievement. Look at setbacks realistically. They usually aren't the end of the world. Learn from failure. What could you have done better? If you think of something, change it. If you did your best, well, that's victory in itself.

You can also build self-esteem by trying something new. Take a chance, and expect a good outcome. Force yourself to be more outgoing. Stop comparing yourself to others. You are "good enough" just the way you are. And stop feeling jealous—yes, you can control that—of what others have. Remember that who you are is more important than what you have. Be grateful for who you are.

CREATIVITY AND CONFIDENCE

Everyone is creative one way or another. Perhaps you haven't discovered your hidden talents. If you're interested in something, it's a sign that you may have a talent for it. Be bold. Explore it. That doesn't mean you must rush out and compose a symphony or write a novel. You can start small and dabble in several activities.

Developing creative hobbies such as photography is another way to increase self-confidence.

Sign up for lessons or workshops. Forgive yourself if you aren't an expert at first. You'll likely have to practice to get better. You don't have to limit yourself to typical "artsy-craftsy" activities like art, music, photography, or writing. You may have a talent for the Hula-Hoop, working with children, tending a garden, or organizing.

The more things you try, the better chance you'll find a creative outlet. Remember you don't have to be perfect to express your creative self. Avoid judging your output. Let yourself have fun doing it.

TRY NEW THINGS

You can build self-esteem simply by doing things. Lots of them. A wide variety of activities adds to your life experience. Participate in school activities. Go to the bonfire. Support school teams by attending games. Join the yearbook staff, chess club, or fashion club. If there's no club for your interests, start one. Attend the youth group at your place of worship. Join a chorus or band.

Invent your own field trips to places of interest in your area—and beyond. Interested in space travel? Plan a trip to space camp. Do you love animals? Help out at pet adoption events. Want to share your musical ability? Hold a summer music camp for the kids in your neighborhood.

THE "WHO AM I?" QUESTIONNAIRE

Sometimes it helps to try something different in order to reflect on yourself in new ways. Filling out a questionnaire is a good way to reflect on preferences, dislikes, points of pride, and dreams. Authors and educators Jack Canfield and Harold C. Wells developed the following questionnaire for students to reflect on themselves in order to develop their self-confidence:

1. In general, school is …
2. I don't like people who …
3. I'm at my best when I …
4. Right now I feel …
6. The best thing that could happen to me is …
7. When I don't like something I've done, I …
8. When I like something I've done, I …
9. When I'm proud of myself, I …
10. I wish my parents knew …
11. Someday I hope …
12. Five adjectives that describe me are …

Ask a parent or teacher to help you arrange to meet professionals in a field you're interested in. You can also volunteer for community work. If you're interested in medicine, volunteer at a hospital. If you love books, see if you can help at the library. Your community has many needs. See what you'd like to do. Look into organizations like Big Brothers and Big Sisters. Coach a youth sports team.

AVOID NEGATIVITY

Some other ways to build self-esteem are under your control. Avoid negative situations. Who needs them? Hang out with positive people whenever you can. Practice saying positive things to others and yourself. If your "friends" always seem to bring you down, change your friends.

Grammy award–winning singer Adele understands. "I've seen people where (appearance) rules their lives, who want to be thinner or have

Singer Adele has publically spoken about the importance of self-esteem to her career—as well as her past struggles getting to a place of confidence today.

87

bigger boobs, and how it wears them down," she told *Rolling Stone*. "And I don't want that in my life. I have insecurities, of course, but I don't hang out with anyone who points them out to me."

Instead, pay attention to the good things in your life. Keep a journal. Write down only positive happenings.

As you participate in new activities, you'll have fun. You'll also find others who share your interests. Some of them may become new friends. You may even develop the sense of belonging that all humans need.

IMPROVING BODY IMAGE

You can also take control of your body image. As with self-esteem, the first step is to stop thinking negative thoughts. If they creep in, switch to a part of the body that you like. Or, think about something else entirely.

For Sara Ramirez of *Grey's Anatomy*, the process is ongoing. "I still have days when I walk by the mirror on my way to the shower and think, 'oh God, I didn't just see that!'" she told *Glamour*. "But I've learned to stop myself and ask, am I being realistic?"

Instead of focusing on your looks, think about the movement that your body lets you do. Are you good at free throws or hip-hop dancing? Do you like bowling or walks in the park? Be grateful for your physical abilities.

Actress Sara Ramirez often speaks of the path to self-confidence as an ongoing process that continues each day.

Ramirez asks herself, "What do I love about my body? What am I grateful for? The answers to those questions remind me that I'm very blessed."

Recognize that your value as a person has nothing to do with your appearance. Stop comparing your body to others'—especially unrealistic television, film, and magazine images you see. Don't compare your body to your peers' either. As a teen, your body is still developing. Different people have different genetic make-ups, as well as different lifestyles, and other environmental factors. Their body changes are likely coming at different times from yours. Consider yourself a work in progress.

Be realistic about what you can change and what you can't. Take steps to change what you can in healthy ways. You can't change your height, eye color, or shoe size. Accept those things. Remember, there is no ideal body type, size, or shape. Instead, accept the diversity. Include yourself. Instead of emphasizing appearance, take responsibility for taking care of your body. Work toward good health.

As you explore ways to build self-esteem and a positive body image, you don't have to go it alone. Life can sometimes seem overwhelming. If you feel that way, ask for help. If that doesn't work—or if your problems are serious—you may need to talk to a professional. Don't hesitate to seek help if you need it.

POSITIVE ROLE MODELS

If you've been misled by media images, look for positive role models outside the stereotypes. Katie Davidson is one. As a high school sophomore she was a place-kicker on the eight-"man" football team at Community Christian School near Atlanta, Georgia.

She was nominated for homecoming queen, but that posed a problem. School rules required girls who were potential members of the homecoming court to wear a dress to the game. Her football uniform didn't qualify. School officials amended the rules to read that the girls had to wear "a dress or football uniform." She was named a homecoming princess.

Sejal Hathi is another teen role model. At age fifteen she founded the international nonprofit organization Girls Helping Girls (GHG) in Fremont, California. The group has helped thousands of girls in more than twenty countries improve their communities, start small businesses, and address global issues.

GHG has raised money to provide computers, school supplies, and scholarships or funding for girls and women to use for education or starting their own businesses. The group also funded a new library in India. In an interview with the *Contra Costa Times*, she said, "Whenever I think of something, I think big."

Sejal Hathi began the nonprofit organization Girls Helping Girls in order to help girls and young women across the globe achieve their dreams.

Hathi coauthored her first book about entrepreneurship at the age of sixteen. She has been recognized by media outlets, organizations, and corporations as well as the US secretary of education and the president of the United States for her academic as well as extracurricular achievements.

But she doesn't call herself a hero. In the *Contra Costa Times* interview, she said,

"My heroes are the millions of girls in developing countries who walk those 10 miles (16 kilometers) to school every day, who have to take care of their siblings every day, who can't go to school, who work on their family farm, who have to get married before age 18 yet still keep on striving, still keep on dreaming, still keep on seeking a better life. Those are my heroes because they teach me that anything is possible and that all human beings are valuable."

TIPS FOR SELF-DEVELOPMENT

The leadership compass developed by PEARLS for Teen Girls provides direction for teens' self-development. The nonprofit leadership development organization in Milwaukee, Wisconsin, helps girls ages ten to nineteen "use their personal power to achieve their dreams and goals."

The five-point compass leads to the self-development of "heart, mind, body, and spirit" that is essential to happiness and well-being. The five points, known as the PEARLS Promise include:

Building relationships with others and helping out in your community are important steps to take in order to develop your own sense of self.

1. **Loving myself:** Believing "I can do it!" Self-appreciation. Taking healthy risks. Building my confidence. Discovering myself.

2. **Building relationships with others:** Appreciating others who are different from me. Trusting the reasons behind what others do. Being understanding of others. Communicating with respect and kindness.

3. **Striving to achieve:** Feeling empowered to make positive decisions in my life. Taking on new leadership roles and responsibilities. Motivating myself to try new, positive things. Working productively in a team environment. Aspire to and envision my ideal future self.

4. **Believing that the sky's the limit:** Being more optimistic about my future. Believing my life has purpose. Finding out about various career options. Building on my talents. Identifying options for my future.

Helping hands in the community: Volunteering my time and talents. Getting involved in a project that addresses a problem. Showing that I care about needs beyond my own neighborhood.

These are great recommendations for any teen who wants to develop their self-confidence and work to build a solid foundation for their future. Believing in oneself is the first step to take before reaching out and developing relationships with others. How you view yourself sets the stage for how others will view and approach you. Develop yourself, focus on achieving your goals, and the sky's the limit for your dreams.

ABUSE Behavior aimed at getting power and control over another person.

ANOREXIA NERVOSA A medical diagnosis for an eating disorder characterized by an intense fear of gaining weight or being fat.

ASSERTIVE COMMUNICATION Social interaction where the parties express both positive and negative feelings in an open, direct way.

BETA-ENDORPHIN A natural body chemical produced in the brain in response to pain, trauma, exercise, or stress.

BINGE EATING Out of control consumption of huge amounts of food.

BODY IMAGE The way you feel about your physical appearance.

BOMBARD To assail someone persistently with questions, criticism, or information.

BULLYING A type of verbal or physical aggression that includes an imbalance of power, intent to harm, and repetition.

CISGENDER Describes a person whose sense of personal identity corresponds with their birth-assigned gender.

CYBERBULLYING Sending embarrassing, false, or harmful messages or images over the internet, mobile phones, or other devices.

DIURETIC A drug or other substance that reduces the amount of water in the body by increasing the amount of urination.

EATING DISORDERS NOT OTHERWISE SPECIFIED (EDNOS) Medical conditions that include combinations of signs and symptoms of anorexia, bulimia, or binge-eating.

INDIRECT AGGRESSION A communication style that is sarcastic, deceptive, or manipulative.

MORPHINE A potentially addictive narcotic pain medication made from opium.

OBESITY A weight more than 20 percent higher than an individual's ideal body weight for his or her height, age, gender, and build.

OBJECTIFICATION Thinking of or presenting something as an object.

PURGING To force consumed food or calories out of the body to keep from gaining weight.

RAMPANT Something, which is usually unpleasant, that spreads widely.

SELF-ESTEEM The way you value yourself.

SELF-INJURY A way to express or relieve pain or punish oneself. It may include cutting, burning, branding, or hitting oneself with an object or against a wall or floor

SEXUALIZATION An emphasis on sexual appeal or behavior in determining self-worth without regard for any other characteristics, such as intelligence or interpersonal skills.

SUBMISSIVE COMMUNICATION Social interaction characterized by a sense of passive helplessness. It may come across as whiny, indecisive, and apologetic.

TOXIC MASCULINITY A term that denotes a criticism of the way certain societies have developed supposedly masculine characteristics to be overly aggressive and dominant.

TRANSGENDER Describes someone whose personal identity does not completely correspond with their birth-assigned gender.

TRICHOTILLOMANIA Hair pulling as a form of self-injury.

American Academy of Nutrition and Dietetics
120 South Riverside Plaza, Suite 2190
Chicago, IL 60606
(800) 877-1600
Website: www.eatright.org
Twitter: @eatright
The American Academy of Nutrition and
Dietetics is a national organization of food
and nutrition professionals formerly known
as the American Dietetic Association. It has
launched several health-based initiatives,
including Kids Eat Right, which aims to end
the childhood obesity epidemic within
one generation.

BullyingCanada
27009–471 Smythe Street
Fredericton, NB E3B 9M1
Canada
(877) 352-4497
Website: www.bullyingcanada.ca
Twitter: @BullyingCanada
BullyingCanada is a registered charity that
connects youth who speak out about bullying
and victimization and who want to help stop
bullying. It is Canada's only national anti-
bullying organization.

Diamond In The Rough (DITR)
2140 McGee Road, Suite C-640
Snellville, GA 30078
(678) 376-9676
Website: www.ditr.org
Facebook: @diamondintheroughinc
Twitter: @DITR_INC
DITR is an award-winning faith-based,
nondenominational organization that
builds self-esteem, character, and leadership
through preventive programs and enrichment
activities. It provides group mentoring,
leadership training, career coaching,
and family enrichment activities for
adolescent girls.

Eating Disorder Hope
207 North Prairie Street
Flandreau, SD 57028
(888) 274-7732
Website: www.eatingdisorderhope.com
Twitter: @EDHope
Eating Disorder Hope is an organization that
provides education and support for both
sufferers of eating disorders and their
families. The group's mission is to develop the
appreciation of each individual's uniqueness
and value, unrelated to appearance.

Girls Action Foundation
   24 Mont Royal West, Suite 601
   Montreal, Quebec H2T 2S2
   Canada
   (888) 948-1112
Website: girlsactionfoundation.ca
Facebook: @girlsaction.fillesdaction
Girls Action Foundation is a Canadian nonprofit
   organization that supports more than three
   hundred organizations and reaches more
   than sixty thousand girls and young women
   through programs that offer empowerment,
   leadership, and community action
   opportunities.

National Association of Anorexia Nervosa and
   Associate Disorders (ANAD)
   800 E Diehl Road #160
   Naperville, IL 60563
   (847) 831-3438
Website: www.anad.org
Facebook: @ANADHelp
ANAD is a national nonprofit organization
   that works to prevent and ease such eating

disorders as anorexia nervosa, bulimia nervosa, and binge eating disorder. It offers treatment referral, support groups, conferences, advocacy, and educational opportunities.

WEBSITES

Due to the changing nature of internet links, Rosen Publishing has developed an online list of websites related to the subject of this book. This site is updated regularly. Please use this link to access the list:

http://www.rosenlinks.com/WITW/Body

Bialik, Mayim. *Girling Up: How to be Strong, Smart and Spectacular.* New York, NY: Philomel Books, 2017.

Bradshaw, Cheryl M. *How to Like Yourself: A Teen's Guide to Quieting Your Inner Critic and Building Lasting Self-Esteem* (The Instant Help Solutions Series). Oakland, CA: Instant Help, 2016.

Brady, Shari. *It's Not What You're Eating, It's What's Eating You: A Teenager's Guide to Preventing Eating Disorders—And Loving Yourself.* New York, NY: Skyhorse Publishing, 2017.

Burgess, Melvin. *Sara's Face.* London, UK: Anderson Press, 2017.

Collins, Lily. *Unfiltered: No Shame, No Regrets, Just Me.* New York, NY: HarperCollins, 2017.

Hemmen, Lucie. *The Teen Girl's Surival Guide; Ten Tips for Making Friends, Avoiding Drama, and Coping with Social Stress* (The Instant Help Solutions Series). Oakland, CA: 2015.

Hilb, Jessie. *The Calculus of Change.* New York, NY: Clarion Books, 2018.

Roberts, Emily, and Jennifer L. Hartstein. *Express Yourself: A Teen's Guide To Speaking Up and Being Who You Are* (The Instant Help Solutions Series). Oakland, CA: Instant Help, 2015.

Scarlet, Janina, and Wellinton Alves. *Superhero Therapy: Mindfulness Skills to Help Teens and Young Adults Deal with Anxiety, Depression, and Trauma.* Oakland, CA: Instant Help, 2017.

Schab, Lisa M. *The Self-Esteem Habit for Teens: 50 Simple Ways to Build Your Confidence Every Day* (The Instant Help Solutions Series). Oakland, CA: Instant Help, 2018.

Schab, Lisa M. *The Self-Esteem Workbook for Teens; Activities To Help You Build Confidence and Achieve Your Goals.* Oakland, CA: Instant Help, 2013.

Sokol, Leslie, and Marci G. Fox. *The Think Confident, Be Confident Workbook for Teens: Activities to Help You Create Unshakable Self-Confidence and Reach Your Goals.* Oakland, CA; Instant Help, 2016.

"Body Image and Nutrition." Teen Health and the Media. Retrieved March 17, 2017. http://www .depts.washington.edu/thmedia/view .cgi?section=bodyimage&page+fastfacts.

"Body Image and Self-Esteem." Teen Health, May 2009. http://kidshealth.org/teen/your _mind/body_image/body_image.html.

Canfield, Jack and Harold C. Wells. *1000 Ways to Enhance Self-Concept in the Classroom.* New York, NY: Allyn and Bacon, 1976. Polk Mentoring Alliance, 2008. https://www.polk -fl.net/community/volunteers/documents /ymConfidenceActivities.pdf.

Center on Media and Child Health. "How Do Magazines Affect Body Image?" Education .com, 2011. http://www.education.com/print/ how-magazines-affect-body-image.

Dove. "The Dove Campaign for Real Beauty." Dove. Retrieved March 17, 2017. http://www .dove.us/Social-Mission/campaign-for-real -beauty.aspx.

Dove. "New Dove Research Finds Beauty Pressures Up, and Women and Girls Calling for Change. PR Newswire, June 21, 2016. http://www.prnewswire.com/news-releases/ new-dove-research-finds-beauty-pressures -up-and-women-and-girls-calling-for -change-583743391.html.

"Eating Disorders Statistics." National Association of Anorexia Nervosa and Associated Disorders. Retrieved March 17, 2017. http://www.anad.org/get-information/about-eating -disorders/eating-disorders-statistics.

Engel, Beverly. *The Nice Girl Syndrome.* Hoboken, NJ: John Wiley & Sons Inc., 2008.

Feigenbaum, Naomi. *Maintaining Recovery From Eating Disorders.* Philadelphia, PA: Jessica Kingsley Publishers, 2012.

Fleming, Olivia. "Was Jennifer Lawrence Too FAT for the Hunger Games? Critics Believe Actress Should Have Looked 'More Hungry.'" *Mail Online,* March 28, 2012. http://www.dailymail .co.uk/femail/article-2121740/Was-Jennifer -Lawrence-FAT-Hunger-Games-Male-critics -believe-actress-looked-hungry .html?ito=feeds-newsxml.

"Healthy Body Image: Tips for Guiding Girls." Mayo Clinic, June 5, 2010. http://www .mayoclinic.com/health/healthy-body-image /MY01225.

Hinde, Natasha. "8 Celebrities Who Opened Up About Eating Disorders." Huffington Post January 11, 2016. http://www. huffingtonpost.co.uk/entry/celebrities- open-up-about-eating-disorders- uk_58187eb8e4b0ccfc9563f0ee.

Lukash, Frederick N. *The Safe and Sane Guide to Teenage Plastic Surgery.* Dallas, TX: BenBella Books, 2010.

Paul, Pamela. "The Playground Gets Even Tougher." *New York Times,* October 8, 2010. http://www.nytimes.com/2010/10/10/fashion/10Cultural.html?pagewanted=all.

Raiten-D'Antonio, Toni. *Ugly As Sin.* Deerfield Beach, FL: Health Communications, 2010.

Silverthorne, Elizabeth. *Anorexia and Bulimia.* Farmington Hills, MI: Lucent Books, 2010.

Swearer, Susan M., Dorothy L. Espelage, and Scott A. Napolitano. *Bullying Prevention and Intervention: Realistic Strategies for Schools,* New York, NY: The Guilford Press, 2009.

Tapper, Christina. "Queen Latifah Achieves Weight-Loss Goal," *People,* June 17, 2008. http://www.people.com/people/article/0,,20207156,00.html.

Wiseman, Rosalind. *Queen Bees and Wannabees: Helping Your Daughter Survive Cliques, Gossip, Boyfriends, and the New Realities of Girl World.* New York, NY: Three Rivers Press, 2009.

Withers, Jennie, and Phyllis Hendrickson. *Hey, Back Off!: Tips for Stopping Teen Harassment.* Far Hills, NJ: New Horizon Press, 2011.

ABOUT THE AUTHORS

Lena Koya is a writer and scholar who writes for both adolescents and adults. She lives in New York with her family and enjoys spending time outdoors and staying healthy by running and practicing yoga.

Mary-Lane Kamberg is an award-winning professional writer specializing in nonfiction for juveniles and adults. She has published twenty-two books, including thirteen for young readers. She is coleader of the Kansas City Writers Group and belongs to the Midwest Children's Authors Guild. She coaches club swimming for the Kansas City Blazers.

PHOTO CREDITS

Cover Studio Grand Ouest/Shutterstock.com; p. 7 Universal Images Group/Getty Images; p. 11 Craig Barritt/Getty Images; pp. 13, 83 Purestock/Thinkstock; p. 19 Brent Harrison/ FilmMagic/Getty Images; p. 23 Bobby Bank/FilmMagic/Getty Images; p. 27 moodboard/Thinkstock; pp. 30-31 Highwaystarz-Photography/iStock/Thinkstock; pp. 34–35 Matt Cowan/ Getty Images; pp. 38–39 DGLimages/iStock/Thinkstock; p. 44 MachineHeadz/iStock/Thinkstock; p. 51 Media for Medical/ Universal Images Group/Getty Images; pp. 52–53 Jason Merritt/Getty Images; p. 55 Ari Perilstein/Getty Images; pp. 58–59 monkeybusinessimages/iStock/Thinkstock; pp. 62–63 Bojan89/iStock/Thinkstock; p. 65 Okea/iStock/Thinkstock; pp. 68–69 CharlieAJA/iStock/Thinkstock; p. 73 Jose Luis Pelaez Inc/Blend Images/Thinkstock; pp. 76–77 Clive Brunskill/Getty Images; p. 81 Ridofranz/iStock/Thinkstock; pp. 86–87 Gareth Cattermole/Getty Images; p. 89 Amanda Edwards/WireImage/ Getty Images; p. 92 Stephen J. Cohen/Getty Images; pp. 94–95 Rawpixel/iStock/Thinkstock; cover and interior pages (globe) LuckyDesigner/Shutterstock.com; cover and interior pages background designs lulias/Shutterstock.com, Dawid Lech/ Shutterstock.com, Transia Design/Shutterstock.com.

Design & Layout: Nicole Russo-Duca; Editor & Photo Research: Elizabeth Schmermund.